# 365
## WINE TIPS

© Front cover pictures: Sopexa (2), Spanish Consulate General (1)

© 2001 DuMont Buchverlag, Köln
(DuMont monte UK, London)

Photographs: CRDO Rueda (2), DWI/Hartmann (3), Heigl & Meyer GmbH (3), Informationsbüro Sherry (2), Informationsbüro Valdepenas (2), Integra Communication (1), Martini (1), Screwpull (2), Sopexa (2), Spanish Consulate General (2)
Translation and typesetting: Rosetta International, London
Manufactured by: Mladinska, Slovenia

ISBN 3-7701-7088-1

Printed in Slovenia

# CONTENTS

# WINE IN HISTORY AND RELIGION

1

There are various theories about the origins of wine. Some believe it originated in an area between Damascus and the mountains of the Caucasus while others think it was somewhere between the Tigris and Euphrates rivers. But experts all agree on one point: it was in some part of the Caucasian region. Although wine is still produced in the area, it is very much on the edge of the international market and it can no longer compete in quality with its descendants in central and southern Europe or those in the New World.

# 2

There is no doubt that it was the Greeks and later the Romans who developed winegrowing in Europe. The Romans introduced winegrowing throughout Europe mainly out of self interest; Caesar's troops did not want to be deprived of their beloved wine when expanding the boundaries and guarding the outposts of the Roman Empire. They therefore took their vines with them and introduced winegrowing into Gaul (France), where the soil and climate were ideally suited.

3

Wine also played a significant part in Greek mythology. The Trojans drank quantities of wine to celebrate their success in holding out for so long against the Greeks. Consequently they fell for Odysseus's ruse of the Trojan horse which enabled the Greeks warriors to enter Troy. The result is well-known: Troy was lost.

# 4

Wine saved the life of the Greek heroes more than once during their ten-year wandering on the seas. The Cyclops Polyphemus became drunk and fell asleep after drinking too much wine, which he had never had before. While asleep, Odysseus blinded him and escaped with his surviving companions from the cave where they were imprisoned.

5

The Romans introduced vines throughout Germany. But these came not from Italy but from Gaul, which was a Roman province long before Germania became one.

6

Wine was not always forbidden on principle by the Muslim religion. At the time of the Prophet, wine was permitted and vines were successfully grown in many Muslim countries. It was only by a revelation later in his life that the consumption of wine in Muslim countries was prohibited and severely enforced by the Mullahs.

**7**

Wine played an important part in most religions. For instance, the Greeks and Romans had their own wine god, Dionysus (Bacchus), a son of Zeus (Jupiter), who introduced winegrowing into many countries throughout the world.

**8**

The religious importance of wine is shown by the fact that during the period of Prohibition in the United States (1919–32), certain winemakers, mainly in California, were allowed to continue producing wine – but only for the celebration of the Eucharist.

# WINE ON THE MOVE

## 9

In the second half of the 19th century, the devastating phylloxera louse travelled from America to Europe, leading to the complete devastation of many European vineyards. To save what could still be saved, many winegrowers "fled" abroad with their remaining healthy vines so as to save at least part of their harvest. A well-known example is that of the French winegrowers from Bordeaux who settled in Navarre and Rioja in Spain.

**10**

Salvation for the European winegrowers came from America in the form of a phylloxera-resistant variety of vine rootstock to which the vines of the Old World were grafted.

**11**

It is the New World that has benefited most from the movement of vines in the last 20 or 30 years. California, South Africa, New Zealand, Australia and Chile have learned from the rich experience of European winegrowers and in many instances overtaken their mentors there. But they have depended on European vines to do so.

Primitivo is a wine variety from southern Italy that has been introduced into California, where it is called Zinfandel. Californian winegrowers have developed this variety into something quite distinctive. It is recognized as the most individual variety of the American West Coast and many growers have created some wonderful wines from it, among them Kent Rosenblum, the "Zinfandel King" who rules from his San Francisco winery.

*13*

The French Syrah grape has also travelled to the other side of the world, Australia. Known there as Shiraz, it is one of the most popular red wine varieties, and Australian winegrowers have interpreted it in a very distinctive way.

*14*

As well as its distinctive varieties, many traditional grape varieties are grown in the New World, including Merlot, Cabernet Sauvignon, Cabernet Franc and Pinot Noir red wine grapes, and Chardonnay, Sauvignon Blanc, Müller-Thurgau, Riesling and Pinot Bianco white wine grapes, to mention just a few.

# WINEMAKING: CARE AND RISKS

## 15

The French term terroir refers to the growing conditions required for a vine to produce the best results: a combination of soil, location, aspect and climate.

# 16

"Training" is the process of supporting and guiding the branches of vines for the best results, using posts, wire and tapes. The most spectacular form is the pergola training used particularly in the hot Mediterranean countries, where the shoots and leaves are trained to form a "roof" over the grapes, protecting them from the heat and preventing the soil drying out.

# 17

The micro-climate can often change the quality and taste of the wine to a considerable degree. Spain for instance is influenced by the Mediterranean and Atlantic, while the South Tyrol and Trentino are affected by the Alps and the Mediterranean. The direction in which a valley lies determines which of these conditions have most effect, whether Mediterranean, Atlantic, or even Alpine.

18

Even fog creates an important micro-climate. Wine-growers in the Napa valley in California welcome the fog that rolls in from the Pacific in the morning, because it provides vital moisture in a region with very little rain.

# 19

Winegrowing is only possible in two zones in the world. In the northern hemisphere, this lies roughly between latitude 30° and latitude 50°. This is where the main traditional winegrowing regions of the world are situated: central and southern Europe, North Africa and the Asian countries where wine has been produced for a very long time. In the southern hemisphere the winegrowing regions lie between latitude 30° and latitude 40° in Chile, Argentina, South Africa, Australia and New Zealand.

# 20

The precise location of a vineyard in a wine region plays a decisive part in the quality of the grapes. The amount of direct sun, the vineyard's height above sea level, the slope of the ground, the distance between the vines, and proximity to rivers or lakes all affect the result.

21

Connoisseurs can often be recognize a wine's terroir from its taste. For instance, wines from particular regions in Australia may have a hint of eucalyptus, since. grapes from vines grown near eucalyptus trees may absorb flavours from the fallen leaves. In most regions the terroir plays decisive part in the wine's classification.

22

For healthy vines and good quality grapes, the soil must be tended to keep it well-drained. The soil is usually cultivated in March, early summer and after the harvest. The planting of other vegetation regulates the nitrogen content in the soil. In California, for instance, grass is planted where necessary between each row of vines, while in Germany it is usually grown between every other row.

**23**

Fertilisers and pesticides – a disturbing thought for environmentalists and purist wine enthusiasts! But two points must be made. In monoculture such as growing vines, the fight against pests and disease is essential. Today this is mainly carried out using biological products. Fertilisers are also necessary to produce a sufficiently large number of grapes of the required quality. But quality-conscious winegrowers use as few chemicals as possible, or even none. Because the natural mould that grows on grapes plays a vital part in the fermentation process, the treatment against damaging moulds must be extremely accurate. and of course no residues must be left in the must.

*Botrytis cinerea* is a desirable mould, known as "pourriture noble" or "noble rot". When this develops on grapes with a particularly high sugar content, they are used to produce first quality (and expensive) dessert wines, such as the world-famous Sauternes and the rare Trockenbeerenauslese wines of Germany and Austria.

# 25

Gene manipulation has also spread to the area of vine growing, particularly with the objective of making vines and their roots resistant to viruses and other pests. However, vines are much harder to manipulate genetically than plants such as soya, for instance.

With the exception of eiswein, the production of grapes for wine takes about six months. In the northern hemisphere the vine-growing season starts in April or May with the appearance of buds and lasts until the harvest or vintage in September or October. But of course this does not mean that the winegrower is idle at other times, since vineyards need attention all the year round.

26

The time of the vintage can also affect the quality of the grapes and in any case the harvest time is different for all grapes. If the grapes are allowed to remain on the vine longer to benefit from the autumn sun and lose part of their moisture content, their sugar content will rise. An early harvest means a lower proportion of sugar.

27

Picking by hand or by machine? Machine-picking is now common, although not possible where the terrain is too steep. But in the case of expensive wines, grapes are always hand-picked even where the land is flat. This is the only way to remove rotten berries and avoid botrytis where it is not desirable. Hand-picking also enables the winegrower to pick the grapes at the perfect stage of ripeness. The vines are picked several times so that only grapes that have reached the perfect degree of ripeness are used.

28

29

Even red grapes produce white wine! This is true when the skins are removed, because the pigment that colours red and rosé wines is contained in the skin. Champagne is of course a white wine, although it consists of two-thirds red grape varieties, for instance, the red Pinot Noir and Pinot Meunier and the white Chardonnay.

# THE WORLD'S MOST IMPORTANT GRAPES

## 30

The same grapes varieties often have different names in different countries. But although they are synonymous, the wine made from them will not be identical everywhere. Differences in climate and winegrowing techniques will usually produce different results, as with Zinfandel in California and Primitivo in Italy.

# 31

**Cabernet Sauvignon**: This red grape variety has a distinctive bouquet of blackcurrants. The typical variety of Bordeaux, it is rich in tannin and is therefore suitable for keeping. It is cultivated all over the world.

**32**

***Cabernet Franc***: This relative of the Cabernet Sauvignon is usually blended with Merlot or Cabernet Sauvignon to produce wines that are fresh and fruity. This variety produces successful wines in California.

***Merlot***: Without Merlot, half of the most famous wines in the world would not exist and even many Bordeaux wines would only be half as interesting without it. Whether as a single variety wine or as part of a blend, the grape variety produces great wines that can be drunk young but can also be kept for a long time. Today Merlot is grown in all the most important wine regions throughout the world.

**33**

***Pinot Noir*:** This is the classic grape variety of Burgundy and it is also grown all over the world. It is known as ***Pinot Nero*** in Italy and ***Blauburgunder*** or ***Spätburgunder*** in Germany and Austria. It is one of the basic grape varieties used to make champagne. So far as taste is concerned, very few wines are so dependant on soil and position as Pinot Noir.

34

# 35

***Pinot Meunier*** is one of the three grape varieties used to make Champagne. Known as ***Schwarzriesling*** or ***Müllerrebe*** in Germany, it is also used there and in Australia as a basis for full-flavoured wines.

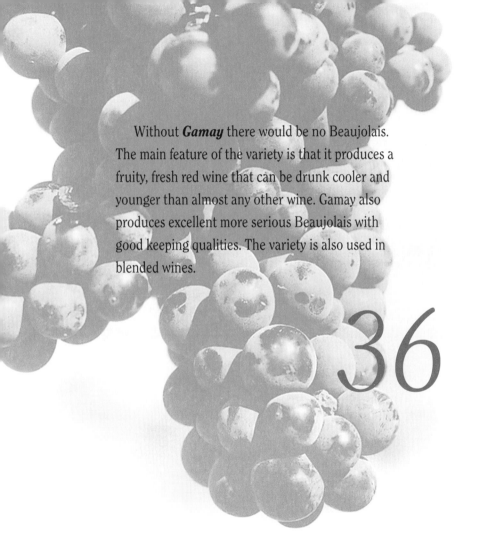

Without **_Gamay_** there would be no Beaujolais. The main feature of the variety is that it produces a fruity, fresh red wine that can be drunk cooler and younger than almost any other wine. Gamay also produces excellent more serious Beaujolais with good keeping qualities. The variety is also used in blended wines.

36

# 37

**Syrah** is the predominant grape variety of the Rhône, and it is an example of a typical French grape variety that has succeeded in becoming virtually a "native" variety everywhere in the world. This is the case especially in Australia where it is known as **Shiraz** and produces powerful, full-bodied wines, often blended with Cabernet Sauvignon and/or Merlot.

38

**Tempranillo** is Spain's best-known red grape variety, used in particular to make Rioja, the Spanish "Bordeaux", which can be produced as an excellent single-variety wine and also as a blended wine. The Reservas and Gran Reservas matured in oak barrels are recognised as some of the best wines in the world. Tempranillo is also grown in Portugal where it is called **Tinta Roriz** or **Aragonez**.

**39**

**Garnacha** is a grape variety native
to Spain. Under the name of **Grenache**,
it is also grown in France, particularly in
the Rhône region, as well as other parts of
the world. It is used mainly to blend with
other grape varieties. As a single variety
wine it is used only to make rosé.

*40*

**Nebbiolo** is the most famous Italian red grape variety. Although it is grown almost everywhere in Italy, it originates in Piedmont where it is used to make some of the best and most celebrated Italian red wines, Barolo and Barbaresco.

**Sangiovese** is the chief grape variety of Tuscany and forms the largest proportion of Chianti. Sangiovese is grown throughout Italy and is also known as **Brunello** and **Calabrese**.

## 42

Besides the main grape varieties there are many others that are only grown in particular regions. For instance, **Marzemino** and **Teroldego Rotaliano** are red grape varieties that are only found in the Trentino and nowhere else in the world.

***Chardonnay*** is probably the best known of the white grape varieties. It is grown almost everywhere in the world and produces a range of very individual wines. Besides being the only white grape variety used in making Champagne, it is also used to make Chablis and the other great white wines of Burgundy.

43

During the 1990s ***Sauvignon Blanc*** came to rival Chardonnay as the most fashionable grape variety. It too is used to make well-known wines such as Sancerre and Pouilly Fumé. This French grape variety is now cultivated very successfully all over the world0, especially in California, Chile, Australia and New Zealand.

**45**

**Pinot Blanc** (known as **Weissburgunder** in Germany and Austria), is also cultivated in many regions of the world. It is widely used in the production of sparkling wine in Germany (Sekt) and Italy.

Many consider **Riesling** the king of white wines. It is a native German variety which is now cultivated in many wine regions throughout the world. Riesling wines are remarkable for their balance of acidity and sweetness, which is why they can be drunk with so many dishes. The best Rieslings are produced in the Rheingau and Moselle regions.

**46**

# 47

The ***Müller-Thurgau*** grape variety (also known as ***Rivaner***) is one of the most famous hybrid varieties. Its parents are the Riesling and Silvaner varieties. It is a popular grape variety which is grown in many wine regions, including much of Europe outside France, England and New Zealand. The wines are lively and best drunk young.

# 48

The **Silvaner** grape variety is native to Germany and Austria and is grown successfully elsewhere, particularly in Alsace. Its wines are particularly popular and good in Franken, the heart of ancient German winemaking.

# 49

**Pinot Gris**, and its synonyms **Pinot Grigio**, **Ruländer** and **Grauburgunder**, was the predecessor of the Chardonnay as a fashionable wine. It is still very popular today. The grape colour varies from nearly black to almost white. In Alsace it is known as **Tokay d'Alsace**.

***Chasselas*** is also known under several names such as ***Gutedel*** in Germany or ***Fendant*** in Switzerland where it is the most important white grape variety.

50

# 51

In spite of its name, ***Welschriesling*** is no relation of the Riesling variety. It has been said that Johann Wolfgang Goethe was also misled when he declared that he always enjoyed a good Riesling – unconfirmed sources report that the wine in question must have been a Welschriesling. But this is unlikely because, as Michael Broadbent head of Sotheby's wine department, has said, it is of "varying quality". Welschriesling is believed to be a grape native to Austria where it is often at its best, but it is also cultivated in the former Yugoslavia where it is known as ***Laski Rizling***.

The **Furmint** grape variety is celebrated as the basic ingredient of Tokay, one of the great dessert wines in the world. Once among the most expensive of all wines, it is now relatively affordable.

52

# 53

The *Muscat* grape – also known as *Moscato* or *Muskateller* depending on the country of origin is – is one of the most popular varieties is also used to make sparkling wines such as Sekt and Asti Spumante. The wines produced from it are increasingly dry. It is not to be confused with the Muscadet of the Loire region which is famous for being the perfect accompaniment to fish-based and seafood dishes.

The **Chenin Blanc** grape is a variety native to the Loire region. It has become an international variety that is cultivated with great success in the New World. In South Africa this robust white grape variety has been given a new name – **Steen**.

54

# 55

The ***Sémillon*** variety is known for its great resistance which is why it is cultivated in so many wine regions. Usually blended with other varieties, such as Chardonnay or Sauvignon Blanc, it is the main component of Sauternes, the exquisite sweet wine from Bordeaux.

# 56

*Trebbiano*, a successful Italian variety, was cultivated and vinified by the Romans. It is an extremely prolific grape variety which is why it is grown almost everywhere in the world. In the south of France, it is called *Ugni Blanc* and without it there would be no Cognac. In California it is known as *St Emilion* and in Australia as *White Shiraz*.

# 57

*Palomino* is a grape variety that thrives on calcareous soil in a hot climate. This is why it is the star variety of Andalusia and one of the main ingredients of sherry. It is also cultivated in many winegrowing regions with similar soil and weather conditions but it has never done as well in other countries as it does in the heat of Andalusia.

**58**

The fragrant *Malvasia* grape variety is one of the oldest in the world and is native to central Italy where it is used to make very refreshing "pearl" or "pétillant" wines.

*Gewürztraminer* is strongly associated with Alsace and it is also cultivated in neighbouring Baden. In both areas this unmistakable grape variety is used to produce some great wines. Although cultivated in the New World, such as in California, attempts to produce wines with the intense taste of those grown in Europe have so far been unsuccesful.

**59**

The **Grüne Veltliner** grape is the celebrated grape variety of Austrian, **Nosiola** is native to the Trentino while **Kerner, Scheurebe** and **Huxelrebe** are typical German grape varieties.

60

# FAMOUS WINES

61

Most wines are blended, consisting of several individual grape varieties. The wine may be identified by the name of the component varieties, but in traditional winegrowing regions it is more common for the wine to carry a name whose use indicates a certain combination of vintages, laid down by the regulations. There are also brands of wines where the wine is produced in large quantity without mark of origin in which the varieties included are rarely mentioned although the vintage may be given.

62

Liebfraumilch is undoubtedly the most famous German wine in other countries. It is a safe but unexciting Rhine wine, brands including "Blue Nun", "Kröver Nacktarsch", "Escherndorfer Lump" and "Zeller Schwarze". The "Viala", "Mederano" and "Yello" labels are also good value for money.

# 63

Barolo is an outstanding wine and one of the best wines in the produced from black grapes. Barolo is made from 100% Nebbiolo grapes and is one of the best ambassadors of its region of origin, Piedmont. This wine will keep for a remarkably long time, about 20 years.

# 64

Next to Barolo, another star among the great Italian red wines is Barbaresco, also from Piedmont and also made from 100% Nebbiolo. The difference between Barolo and Barbaresco is due to the terroir: the region where Barbaresco is produced being drier and warmer. Barbaresco is excellent value for money.

Sassicaia is probably the most expensive Italian wine. Made in Tuscany, it consists of two-thirds Cabernet Sauvignon and one-third Cabernet Franc. Hugh Johnson described it as a pioneering development by the winery that created it.

65

Edelzwicker is even more closely associated with Alsace than Gewürztraminer. It is a blend made from several grape varieties, the main ingredients being Chasselas and Sylvaner.

66

Frascati is likely to have been the first Italian wine enjoyed by visitors to the country in the 1950s. It remains very popular in the pizzerias of the capital. The wine is produced to the south of Rome and consists mainly of Malvasia and Trebbiano.

67

# 68

Kalterersee is an excellent red wine made from Vernatsch, the typical grape variety of the Alto Adige. Unfortunately it was originally produced as a cheap wine, sold in a two-litre bottle, which probably did its image no good. But that was a long time ago and has long been forgotten. Only 20 communes around Bolzano and in the Trentino are allowed to produce Kalterersee wines.

# 69

One of the few white Bordeaux wines is Sauternes, a sweet wine that is famous throughout the world. It is made from a blend of Sémillon, Sauvignon Blanc and Muscadelle. The most famous Sauternes is Château d'Yquem.

70

"Opus One" is the creation of two of the most famous winegrowers in the world, Robert Mondavi of the Napa Valley and Baron de Rothschild of Bordeaux. It is one of the greatest red wines produced in California and is made from 100% Cabernet Sauvignon. It sells for extremely high prices in the best restaurants of the world and in the famous auction houses of London and New York.

# WINE AND SPARKLING WINE AS APERITIFS AND AFTER MEALS

In stores, sherry is normally found in the vicinity of spirits although they have nothing in common. Being fortified, the alcohol content is higher than ordinary wine. Nonetheless, sherry is itself a wine, being fermented, rather than a spirit, which is distilled to achieve a very high level of alcoholic strength.

71

# 72

Sherry should be recognised as much more than a drink that only comes in three versions, sweet, medium and. dry. This wine from Andalusia comes in many forms and colours. As well as the very dry Manzanillos and Finos, there is also dry Amontillados, dry Olorosos (which also be slightly mellow) as well as the very sweet Pedro Ximenez which "stands" in the glass like oil and is a perfect accompaniment to so many puddings. In addition to these differences in sweetness, sherry is also classed according to quality.

# 73

Manzanilla and Fino are the driest sherries, Fino being by far the most popular type in Spain. Manzanilla must come from the small town of San Lucar de Barrameda on the Spanish Atlantic coast, some 25 km (16 miles) from Jerez. Besides being excellent aperitifs, both sherries can also be drunk with fish and seafood dishes.

# 74

The traditional Amontillados and Olorosos are dry sherries. Oloroso does not develop the flor yeast that is characteristic of Finos and Amontillados while they mature. They are popular for drinking "between meals" or simply as an aperitif.

# 75

Cream sherry is made from Oloroso and the sweetest grape variety of Andalusia, Pedro Ximenez. Naturally Pedro Ximenez is made from the grape variety of the same name (abbreviated to PX). But the main grape variety used to produce sherry is Palomino. Sweet sherry is an ideal dessert wine or digestive. The advantage of both these types of sherry over cognac and whisky is that they contain much less alcohol.

# 76

The temperature at which these fortified wines from southern Spain are drunk is very important. While Manzanilla and Fino should be drunk cold (even from the refrigerator), the cold would destroy the delicate taste of Amontillado and Oloroso, which are drunk at room temperature like red wine.

White wines can also be drunk as aperitifs, as long as they are not too sweet. But it also depends on the food to be eaten later. Whether the aperitif is wine, Campari, Martini or other, it is the alcohol that stimulates the appetite, not the elements that provide the taste. In this light, it could be said that any alcoholic drink may be offered as an aperitif. However, spirits and some wines may affect the taste buds too much to allow the first course to be enjoyed properly.

77

78

The most popular aperitifs are sparkling wines such as Champagne. Check that the label mentions the words "Brut" or "Extra Dry", since semi-dry wines should be avoided as an aperitif.

Drinks are described as "fashionable" when a large part of the population who go out – chiefly the young – favour the same drink so that it becomes commonly available in every pub and restaurant. Unfortunately, when a product becomes over-subscribed it often leads to a reduction in quality.

# 80

An example is the Italian sparkling wine Prosecco in Germany, which has achieved the status of a "fashionable" wine, often served by the glass in pubs and restaurants. This will lead any wine connoisseur to wonder how the winegrowers in this small region between Conegliano and Valdobbiadene, situated in the northern province of Treviso are able to produce this wine in such large quantities.

The method of production means that Champagne is inevitably expensive. But it is worth tasting different brands by the well-known houses – the most expensive is not necessarily the best. Indeed, some of the less expensive "own brand" Champagnes sold in supermarkets may be very satisfactory.

82

It is unusual but possible for even first-quality vintage champagne to be corked, that is, to suffer from cork taint. In that case, the bottle must be taken back to the wine merchant or supplier as soon as possible.

# 83

When sparkling wine is produced by the traditional method, the méthode champenoise, it is always mentioned on the label. In Italy, this type of wine is known as Spumante and Talento (metodo tradizionale), in Germany as Sekt and in Spain as Cava.

## 84

Most dry white wines can be drunk as aperitifs, including the fashionable wines of the last two few years, Chardonnay, the wine of the 1990s, and Sauvignon Blanc, the wine of today. A light Riesling is also ideal. Most of these wines can then be served with the rest of the meal where white wine is indicated.

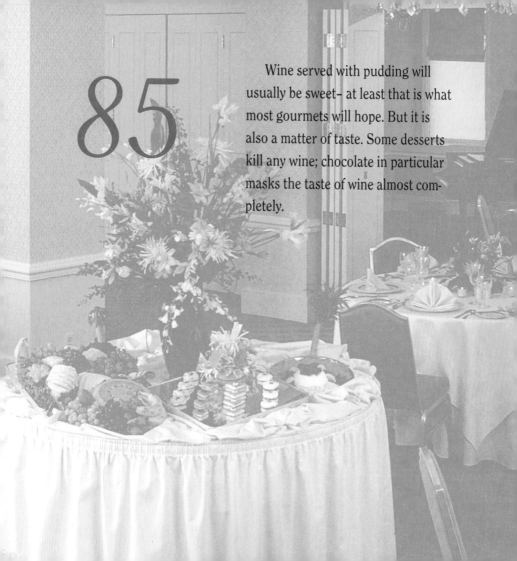

85

Wine served with pudding will usually be sweet– at least that is what most gourmets will hope. But it is also a matter of taste. Some desserts kill any wine; chocolate in particular masks the taste of wine almost completely.

Sweet wines are expensive not only because they are rare but also because they are very costly to produce. The grapes are hand-picked, almost one by one, so that they can be selected at their peak. This is when the grapes are almost dry, in fact almost raisin-like. Alternatively they they may be spread out on wooden racks and dried. Either way, the result is that the sugar content of the small amounts of remaining must is very high. Examples are Sauternes (France), Trockenbeerenauslese, Eiswein (Germany), Ausbruch (Austria), Vino Santo (Italy, Spain).

86

# 87

Sweet wine is also delicious with cheese. There is a cheese manufacturer in Austria who produces a cheese matured with noble rot sweet wine. The name of the cheese reflects the quality of the sweet wine used to refine it: Grand Cru.

88

Cigars and wine: In spite of all information to the contrary, this is not a combination to be reommended. The wine would have to be incredibly strong-flavoured to compete with the strength of a Havana cigar. A strong "digestif" would be more suitable although even here the taste buds might be affected.

## 89

Champagne is the one wine that is traditionally thought to be suitable for drinking throughout the meal, although the price might make this a difficult course to follow.

# THE WORLD OF
# SPARKLING WINES

*90*

Champagne is a wine produced
with great care and it deserves special treatment. It does this noble
drink no favours to be served in a
plastic beaker, as sometimes happens
with some airlines.

## 91

Champagne can be ruined after a few hours if it is badly stored, so it should always be bought from a trustworthy source.

## 92

Like other wines, Champagne should be stored at a constant temperature in a cellar or a cupboard with controlled temperature.

# 93

Wine "breathes" through the cork, so it should not be stored in the same place as strong-smelling substances such as fuel oil. Wherever the wine is stored, the area should be aired from time to time.

# 94

Light is also an important factor. Champagne should be stored in complete darkness. Both the heat of the light fitting and the light itself can damage the wine if the bottle is placed in its immediate vicinity.

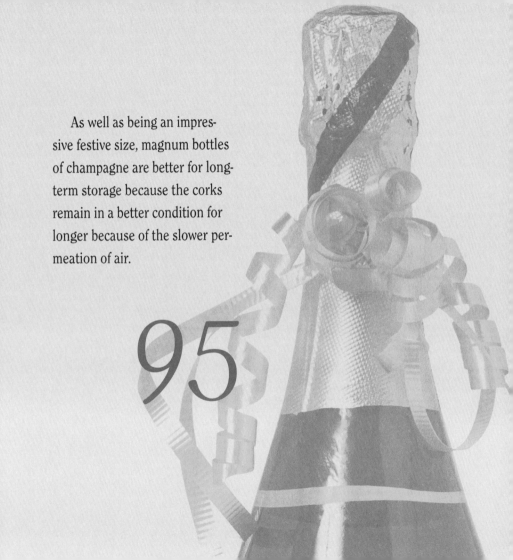

As well as being an impressive festive size, magnum bottles of champagne are better for long-term storage because the corks remain in a better condition for longer because of the slower permeation of air.

95

96

Champagne must be chilled before being served. The bottle should be refrigerated for at least five hours before it is opened. If unexpected guests arrive the chilling process can be accelerated by placing the bottle in the freezer compartment. Contrary to popular belief, this does harm the wine – but remember to remove it before it freezes.

97

When champagne glasses are stored in a wooden cabinet it is said that they absorb some of the smell of the furniture, which spoils the taste of the champagne.

A simple trick to remove the smell of wood is to wave the glasses vigorously in the air. Rinsing in water is also effective.

98

With older vintage Champagne, the cork is sometimes so tight that it is very hard to remove. The best technique for removing any champagne cork is to hold the cork and twist the bottle, rather than the other way round. If the cork still refuses to come out, some form of wrench may have to be used, although this is not a very elegant solution.

99

# 100

If the champagne does not
react with a pop when the cork is removed it
means that the carbon dioxide has escaped.
This Champagne will be flat and is no longer
very pleasant.

*101*

What is the best glass for Champagne or any
other sparkling wine? A goblet or flute.

The traditional saucer-like glass is not recommended. and is now fortunately almost a thing of the past. The bubbles and bouquet would dissipate as soon as the champagne was poured out.

102

# 103

The bubbles play an important part in the enjoyment of Champagne because they are refreshing and also because they seem to accelerate the pleasant effect of drinking the wine.

When there is too little fizz it is not usually because of the age of the Champagne but because the glass has not been rinsed properly. A tiny amount of grease or detergent will reduce the bubbles.

104

# 105

A bottle of champagne that has been opened can easily survive two days in the refrigerator losing none of its fizz so long as it is sealed with a special top designed for sparkling wine.

# 106

Champagne cocktails are abhorred by purists, who argue that it is a pity to contaminate the taste of champagne with other ingredients. For such purposes, less exotic sparkling wines may be used.

The classic "Champagne Cocktail" consists of a dash of angostura on a lump of sugar put in the glass, over which Champagne is poured and a twist of lemon added. The "Prince of Wales" has a dash of Angostura on a lump of sugar to which ice, a slice of orange, brandy, Benedictine and Champagne are added. The well-known "Bellini" created by Harry's Bar in Venice is made from Prosecco, puréed white peach and a few drops of lemon juice. A "Kir royal" is made of crème de cassis and Champagne. Other popular drinks are Buck's Fizz (orange juice and Champagne), and Black Velvet (Guinness and Champagne), in both cases 50:50.

# 108

Pink champagne is also popular for its attractive colour. It is made by blending a little red wine with normal Champagne.

*109*

Some purists disapprove of pink champagne, yet Dom Perignon, the most famous vintage champagne produced by the Moët & Chandon, is also available as pink champagne.

**110**

There is no way in which red champagne could be made. This is because during the remuage stage, when the bottles are inverted and periodically twisted, it would be impossible to see through the opaque wine when the yeast plug had reached the neck of the bottle.

**111**

Champagne made from white grapes only is called "Blanc de Blancs".

# 112

Crémant is also a Champagne but it has less fizz than "normal" Champagne.

Champagne (and some other wines) come in bottles of various sizes, with approximate capacities as follows: **quarter-bottle**: 187 ml/6⅜ fl oz; **half-bottle**: 375 ml/ 12¾ fl oz; **bottle** 750 ml/25⅜ fl oz; **Magnum**: 2 bottles, 1.5 litres (⅖ US gal); **Jereboam**: 4 bottles, 3.0 litres (⅘ US gal); **Rehoboam**: 6 bottles, 4.50 litres/1 Imp. gal (1⅕ US gal); **Methuselah**: 8 bottles, 6.00 litres/ 1½ Imp. gal (1⅗ US gal); **Salmanazar**: 12 bottles, 9.00 litres/2 Imp. gal (2⅖ US gal) ; **Balthasar**: 16 bottles, 12.00 litres/22/3 Imp. gal (3⅕ US gal); and **Nebuchadnezzar**: 20 bottles, 15.00 litres/ 3⅓ Imp.gal (4 US gal).

# 113

There are other excellent sparkling wines produced in other countries such as Spumante and Talento in Italy and Cava in Spain. These classy sparkling wines are made from native grapes, usually following the traditional méthode champenoise.

# 115

The best sparkling wine in Germany is Winzersekt ("winegrowers' sekt"), which is becoming increasingly popular. They are usually made from one grape variety following the traditional méthode champenoise.

# 116

Asti Spumante has always been synonymous with Italian sparkling wine. It is made from Muscat grapes grown in Piedmont. In spite of its high sugar content, Moscato d'Asti is a very refreshing sparkling wine.

**117**

Moët & Chandon and many other labels belong to the LVMH luxury group (Louis Vuitton-Moët-Hennessy).

The oldest champagne house is Ruinart, founded in 1729.

**118**

119

The largest winery making sparkling wine is owned by the Spanish Cava producers Codorniú. It uses caves consisting of tunnels 35 km (22 miles) long under the Panades mountains near Barcelona, equipped with an electric train.

Champagne's popularity through the ages among royal houses, leading restaurants and high society is unrivalled. It is said that Joe DiMaggio conquered Marilyn's Monroe's heart by presenting her with a bath tub filled with Champagne. This would have required between 200 and 300 bottles.

*120*

# WINE TASTING, CARE AND STORAGE

*121*

The study of wine is a very specialised discipline and wine tasting requires specific skills. There are characteristic features of taste and bouquet by which individual wines are assessed. In the case of blended wines, this is more difficult because several grape varieties are involved.

# 122

Typical white wine bouquets:

**Fruity**: These may include tropical (banana, pineapple, mango etc.), artificial fruit (boiled sweets), cooked fruit (apple or pear compote) and dried fruit (dried apricots or raisins).

**Floral**: Jasmine or lilac, vegetable (mint, grass, green beans, asparagus etc.).

Spicy: Lavender, eukalyptus.

Smoky: resinous, tar-like.

123

Typical red wine bouquets:
**Fruity** (berries, stone fruits, citrus fruits, artificial and cooked fruit as well as dried fruit). There are also **floral** and **spicy** bouquets.

*124*

Taste characteristics are based on a set of recognized criteria, but wine tasting is inevitably a subjective matter. The biggest mistake is to rely uncritically on a wine expert's conclusions. When tasting wine the first question one should ask oneself is whether one likes it or not.

Extreme and fanciful descriptions of taste and bouquet such as cat's urine, leather saddles, oyster shells and baked cheese topping are sometimes encountered, but for most people they have little to do with wine tasting in the real world.

*125*

It is almost impossible to provide universal criteria and guidelines for judging wine, since individual tastes and external circumstances on which any assessment is based are too variable. But some suggestions can be made.

*126*

# 127

There are a few simple rules that can help wine enthusiasts to find their way in the jungle of the wine market.

128

One should be cautious when following the judgements of influential wine writers, because while their advice may be sound, their influence may increase the price by more than is justified by the quality, so that it may no longer be worth it.

**129**

It may be more effort to find superb wines among the many on offer in the retail trade or specialist shops, but it will hit be much less expensive and better value than taking the easier course of buying an expensive top-of-the-range wine.

**130**

Wine warehouses and discount stores sell wines which may be excellent value so do not be put off by the cardboard boxes of these sometimes cheerless places. Some wine warehouses have bottles open for tasting.

_131_

Naturally price is an important criterion when buying wine. But it is worth remembering that the level of fixed costs for the bottle and transport (plus UK duty) are much the same for any wine, so at the lower price levels a small increase in price may buy a much greater increase in quality, since it may double the amount spent on the wine itself.

Champagne is expensive because it is labour-intensive and costly to produce. It is also  subject to strict production rules.

# 133

Rare red wines, especially those from Bordeaux, are also extremely expensive. This is due not only to their rarity but also the high production costs (for instance, the grapes are hand-picked so that any rotten grapes are avoided.) The wines of Burgundy such as Chablis are expensive because of the small size and therefore production of the region.

*134*

A Chablis, for instance, comes from a specific area, so it will always tend to be more expensive than a generic Chardonnay, and within the Chablis appellation quality and price will vary.

## 135

However, caution is recommended because consumers are often prepared to pay more for a wine simply because the label bears the name of a picturesque vineyard.

## 136

Wines from the United States are often surprisingly expensive, with prices in some cases exceeding those of the top vineyards of Europe. The main reasons include the laws of supply and demand, and the fact that achieving quality is inevitably costly.

Europeans holidaying in the United States should refrain from buying wine there because vintage wines are usually less expensive in Europe. But the cost of transport in small quantities may cancel out the theoretical advantage for Americans buying in Europe.

137

# 138

As soon as a bottle of wine has been opened, experts will be able to tell whether a wine is good or not on the basis of several criteria. Even the label will tell the drinker quite a few things about the wine such as the region, place of origin, grape variety, wine-producer and quality.

# 139

Some defects are not hard to establish from the bottle. For instance, it is easy to see if the wine is cloudy or if there is a visible alteration in its appearance. This is usually a sign of oxidation, meaning that oxygen has got inside the bottle through a defective or old cork.

## 140

One of the most serious defects in a wine is a corked taste, smelling like a musty, mouldy cellar. Caused by a diseased cork, such a wine is definitely not pleasant to drink.

Another thankfully much rarer defect is when the wine smells of rotten eggs, caused by the sulphur dioxide used in making the wine turning to hydrogen sulphide. Often this unpleasant smell disappears of its own accord after a time.

## 141

142

The nasty effect of hydrogen sulphide can also be "expelled" by a placing a copper coin in the wine because copper reacts with the hydrogen sulphide to make copper sulphate, thsu removing the cause of the smell.

Any wine with a smell and taste of vinegar should be rejected. It is the result of the alcohol turning to acetic acid.

143

# 144

A woody taste sometimes develops in a wine when a barrel has not been cleaned properly. This normally refers to the large barrels in which fermentation takes place, rather than barriques. Sometimes, completely new, unused barriques can produce casky wine.

145

Small crystals forming on the cork, at the bottom of the bottle or in the glass in cold weather are tartaric acid. They are natural and harmless, and do not influence the quality of the wine in any way.

# 146

Wine sometimes has a metallic taste, which is caused by the use of metal objects or tools – especially old tools – during the vinification process. The stainless steel tools and vats widely used today do not cause a metallic taste in the wine.

# 147

Sediment occurs only in red wines; it is the residue that develops and builds up in the bottle over the years as it ages. So it is found in vintage wines that have been laid down, such as Bordeaux, Burgundy and in particular Port. It is not a defect in the wine, but it does mean that these wines should be decanted before serving: in other words, they should be poured carefully and slowly into a glass carafe, stopping as soon as the sediment reaches the neck of the bottle.

To find out which vintages will keep, and more importantly improve, over a long period, the advice of a specialist wine shop should be sought, or the many wine magazines and reference works consulted.. It is important to have a suitable storage space, such as a cellar or temperature-controlled cupboard. Alternatively a wine merchant will store wine for customers for an annual charge.

148

# 149

In principal red wine will keep for
several years if it contains enough tannin because the latter breaks down very
slowly. Red wine matured in barriques
acquires an additional "dose" of tannin
from the wood. The capacity to improve
when laid down depends above all on
the quality of the vintage.

## 150

White wine will also keep for a long time but not as long as the great red wines.

## 151

Sparkling wines usually have a shorter lifespan than still white wines or red wines. Champagne will often be much improved by being kept it for a year or two, but there is little benefit thereafter. Vintage champagne will mellow with age.

# 152

In the right- but not necessarily practical - conditions, Champagne can keep for a
surprisingly long time; the contents of a few
bottles discovered in a ship that sank near
Norway at the end of the 19th century were
still intact and drinkable.

## 153

There are three crucial aspects to be taken into account in assessing wine: colour, bouquet and taste.

## 154

The colour of white wine ranges from almost colourless to amber; any darker usually indicates a fault with the wine. Red wines range from almost pink to dark red. The colour gives an approximate idea of the age of the wine. Near-colourless or watery white wine indicates that it is a young wine while dark yellow indicates it is an older wine. In the case of red, the purple colour of youth tends towards brick red with age.

*155*

Bouquet is the second criterion. It informs about the structure of the wine as well as its origin, reflected in quite specific properties.

*156*

Taste is the third criterion. The body, sweetness, acidity, maturity and level of alcohol are determined by the tongue, which has four areas for different kinds of taste: sweet (tip of the tongue), bitter (at the back of the palate), acidic and salty (on both sides).

When tasting wine, the glass should be only about a quarter full, so that it leaves enough room to swirl the wine. This causes oxygen to be absorbed by the wine, enabling the bouquet to develop fully.

**157**

**158**

In tasting, wine is "chewed" to stimulate their taste buds, so as to acquire a comprehensive impression of the wine.

# 159

The "legs" remaining on the sides of the glass after swirling the wine are an indication of its glycerine content. This is an indication that the wine was made from well-ripened grapes. It also shows the good quality, especially of red wine.

The gustatory substances present in the wine are what determines which wine combines best with which food. The traditional rules of red meat with red wine and white meat with white wine are a guide but not an irrevocable edict – there are plenty of exceptions.

In restaurants, the chef and wine waiter work together when creating a menu. For instance, the content of the sauce should be taken into account when advising on wine. The same is true at home.

It is a mistake to use a poor wine for cooking. It should at least be good enough to drink. Why should a dish be cooked with a wine that is undrinkable? However, it would naturally be a waste to use the finest wine in the cooking process, which will inevitably destroy most of the aspects that make it great.

162

163

It is not the alcohol in wine that adds to the flavour of food in the pan. In fact, it evaporates very quickly at cooking temperatures. It is the essential substances, tannin, acids and sugars contained in the wine that add the flavour to the dish.

The art of choosing the perfect wine lies in ensuring that the bouquet and taste suit the various components of a dish, instead of conflicting with it. Another good guide in the case of a regional dish is to partner it with a wine from the same region.

164

# 165

A common misapprehension is that sherry, champagne and sparkling wines are only drunk as aperitifs, and sweet wines as a digestive at the end of the meal. In Andalusia, sherry and its variations (such as Montilla) is drunk like a wine.

Champagne is also suitable for drinking with a meal - however, its price may counsel against this.

**166**

**167**

White wine is usually drunk with fish, shellfish and crustaceans but it also depends in a large measure on the preparation. For instance, some grilled fish (not oily) can also take a light red wine.

Seafood almost cries out for Champagne. Oysters (said to be an aphrodisiac) and Champagne are a match made in heaven.

168

169

Caviar and Champagne is a legendary – on Concorde it was included in the price of the ticket. But not everyone finds this an ideal combination – the harmony between the most elegant of wines and the salty eggs of the sturgeon is questionable, but naturally it is a matter of taste.

# 170

Seafood need not always be washed down with Champagne; a very dry Muscadet or Chardonnay – especially Chablis – is also delicious with seafood.

# 171

An Italian wine is the obvious accompaniment for pasta dishes. The choice of wine will depend on the sauce accompanying the pasta. For instance, white wine is delicious served with spaghetti alle vongole (with clam sauce) while a Chianti is better suited to meat and other strong-tasting sauces such as the spicy penne arrabiata (with hot pepper).

Gewürzrtraminer or Riesling are good wines to accompany Thai, Vietnamese, Chinese and Japanese dishes. The traditional accompaniment is of course sake (rice wine).

# 172

In the case of meat, the choice of wine depends almost entirely on the sauce. For instance, veal, pork and lamb as well as poultry can be served with white wine, so long as the sauce is light-coloured. Beef and venison demand powerful red wines such as Burgundy, Bordeaux or Rhône wines, or equivalent varietals such as Cabernet-Sauvignon or Merlot, Pinot Noir and Syrah (Shiraz).

The wine served with the pudding naturally depends on what it is. Sweet wines come to mind immediately. But this would not be right with ice-cream or sorbet, for instance. In this case, Champagne or another sparkling wine would be much better.

Port is said by some to be good with puddings containing chocolate because the fortified wine "penetrates" the film deposited by the chocolate on the tongue and palate.

175

176

Fresh fruit and sparkling wine go very well together.

# 177

Sweet white "pudding" wines, such as Sauternes and Beaumes de Venise from France, Trockenbeerenauslese and Eiswein from Germany and Vin Santo from Italy have become very fashionable in the last few years. Some of these are rare and therefore expensive.

**178**

Exotic meats are become increasingly popular. Here wine from the same country is a good starting point, such as Australian with kangaroo steaks or South African with ostrich. Whether red or white depends on the dish and how it is prepared.

**179**

The harmony between food and wine is very important because it influences the digestion. For this and other reasons, it is widely thought that wine consumed in moderation has a positive effect on health.

# WINE AND HEALTH

There is a natural harmoy between food and wine, which is also beneficial to digestion. Wine is believed to have a good effect on health – so long as it is drunk in moderation, of course.

180

# 181

A "unit" of alcohol is the amount in a 125 ml/4 fl oz (½ cup) glass of wine with a strength of 8% alcohol. This is an unusually low level of alcoholic strength, found only in some German wines. Most wine is in the range of 11% to 13% alcohol. A glass of 12% wine will contain 1.5 units of alcohol.

*182*

It is advised that the maximum daily intake of alcohol should be 21 to 35 units per week for men and 14 to 21 for women. The amount varies with body weight. The maximum advised quantities of 12% wine are equivalent to 2–3 glasses a day for men and 1⅓–2 glasses per day for women.

*183*

But when driving, the smallest amount of alcohol (even below the legal limit) is known to impair judgement and increase reaction times.

184

Red wine is said to be healthier than white wine, although this has not been proved conclusively. The "health-promoting" features of red wine are possibly due to the presence of tannin and extracts that are absent in white wine.

*185*

In antiquity, red wine was perceived as a medicinal remedy. It was recommended for headaches by Hippocrates – supposedly diluted with water. The scientific reason for this is that alcohol stimulates blood circulation.

Alcohol's property of stimulating blood circulation is used in medicine today. There is a spray consisting of over 80% alcohol carried by patients with a high risk of suffering a cardiac infarction.

*186*

# 187

Wine stimulates the kidneys as well as the thyroid gland.

But which wine should you choose, from a health point of view? In general, red wine because it is less acidic than white.

# 188

# 189

Wine has also been shown to have a positive effect on blood cholesterol levels.

# 190

How can a hangover be cured? There is no guaranteed method. It is easier to avoid it in the first place...

## 191

A piece of discredited advice is to take "the hair of the dog that bit you", that is, to start the day with the same drink that you ended the evening with. This is nonsense - and a glass of whisky for breakfast is surely unthinkable!

## 192

Many people swear by beer or wheat (white) beer. This may calm the stomach but what about the head? It is best to steer clear from alcohol in the morning.

Aspirin and similar remedies give temporary relief to a headache but as soon as their effect has worn off, you may well feel hung-over again.

*193*

*194*

But what will help most is drinking as much water as possible. Alcohol has a dehydrating effect, so water returns the body to its normal equilibrium.

## 195

There are some preventive measures you can take such as drinking milk before drinking alcohol. This will create a protective layer in your stomach.

## 196

Another word of advice is not mix your drinks, particularly grape (wune) and grain (spirits). This can have unpleasant results remarkably quickly.

# 197

Miracle cures such as a "Bloody Mary" only have a temporary pick-me-up effect that is largely illusory.

## 198

Red wine and in particular port cause more uncomfortable "morning-after" effects than white. This is because they contain volatile esters.

## 199

The medicinal benefits of wine are well seen in Mediterranean countries where people of advanced age are often seen sitting at café terraces enjoying their red wine.

# 200

Wine is only one part of the explanation for the health and long life of Mediterranean people. Their diet is very healthy, with olive oil, fresh vegetables and fruit, and their laid-back, relaxed nature keeps them free of stress.

It is the combination of a Mediterranean diet and wine that is beneficial to health. This has been widely recognized all over the world.

201

# 202

Famous, expensive vintages are beyond the reach of most people for everyday drinking. In the southern parts of Europe where the average income is low, the local "vin de pays" (wine of the country) has long been the norm.

# WINE CLASSIFICATION

**203**

Vins de pays (wine of the country) can be excellent wines and deservedly they are becoming increasingly popular. But the regulations governing their production are becoming increasingly strict.

**204**

Many vins de pays (wine of the country) and vins de table (table wine) and their equivalents in other countries, in other words the category below the various appellations of origin, are still much undervalued. Of course some regional wines are less sophisticated, just tasting nice and pleasant to drink.

# 205

Wines often seem to taste much better in their country of origin than at home. One reason for this is that even less good wine will taste extremely pleasant in a holiday atmosphere.

# 206

The wine that seemed so delicious on holiday may be rather disappointing when you are back home and open a bottle to enjoy with your friends.

# 207

Besides the wine's origin, a wine label may also mention the name of the winegrower, alcohol content, grape variety (if the wines are not blended), quantity and vintage, plus further information laid down by the country of origin or other authorities – sometimes to the winegrower's irritation. The intention is standardize the information and readability of labels so that comparisons can be made.

There are table wines in almost all winegrowing countries and everywhere they are the "lowest category". This does not reflect their quality; the category includes wines whose composition does not meet the grape varieties specified by the appellation, and these can be very remarkable indeed. Only native grape varieties can be used to make table wine. The place of origin only refers to the entire region and not to particular places.

208

## 209

In France, table wine is called "vin de table", in Italy "vino di tavola", in Spain "vino de mesa", in Portugal "viñho de mesa" and in Greece "epitrapezios".

## 210

German and Austrian wine laws are rather different. The simplest designation is "Landwein" (vin de pay) or Tafelwein (vin de table), but this describes wine made from less-ripe grapes, and in another year riper grapes from the same vineyard would earn a higher designation.

## 211

The equivalents of the French "vin de pays" are as follows: in Italy "vini di tavola indicazione geografica tipica" ("IGT"), in Portugal "vinhos regionais", in Spain "viño comercial" and in Greece "topicos oinos".

In Germany and Austria, the category above
"Landwein" (vin de pay) or Tafelwein (vin de table) is
"QbA", "Qualitätswein vestimmter Anbaugebiete",
which means "quality wine from a given area".

212

*213*

In Germany, the label must carry an official test number, "AP" or "Amtliche Prüfungsnummer" and the stipulated minimum degree of ripeness ("Oechsle").

In France the superior categories are AC, "Appellation Contrôlée" and AOC, "Appellation d'Origine Contrôlée". In Italy they are DOC, "Denominazione di origine controllata" and DOCG, "Denominazione di origine controllata garantita". For the area in question, these stipulate the grape varieties to be used and the yield permitted as well as the minimum maturation period and tasting provisions.

214

# 215

Spain has DO, "Denominación de origen" and Portugal has I. P. R. = Indicaçao de Proveniencia Regulamentada). The regulations in these countries are similar to those of Italy and France but slightly less strict.

# 216

The Greeks have similar systems to those of the other European winegrowing countries. The letters OPAP on the label indicate a category similar to a French appellation.

217

The highest category in Germany is QmP, "Qualitätswein mit Prädikat". The "ladder" of Qualität with Kabinett, up to Spätlese, Auslese, Beeren- and Trockenbeerenauslese and finally up to Spezialität Eiswein in which the grapes have been affected by the first frosts.

# 218

In Austria, there is an additional level between Beerenauslese and Trockenbeerenauslese, "Ausbruch", which is made from hand-picked, over-ripe berries with noble rot.

219

Another interesting wine in Austria is "Strohwein" or "straw wine". The berries are dried on straw or reed mats for at least three months.

France divides its top wines – AOC – into several different complicated classification such as the five categories of "Crus classés" or classed growths of Bordeaux.

220

# 221

Italy also has another classification above DOC, namely DOCG, "Denominazione di origine controllata e garantita". These include areas such as Barolo, Barbaresco, Brunello di Montalcino, Chianti Classico and so on.

222

In Spain the highest category is DOCa , "Denominación de origen califica-da". This category is subjected to the most stringent regulations.

# 223

California itself does not have a formal classification system. What matters most with Californian wines is the name of the domain or winegrower.

The United States as a whole has over 100 "Approved Viticultural Areas" (AVA), of which over half are in California. But these only differentiate between "wines made from particular grape varieties" and "type wines", such as "Bordeaux", "Burgundy", "Moselle" and so on. The criteria are not comparable to those used in Europe.

224

**225**

California, Oregon and Washington State account for 95% of United States wines.

**226**

There are labels in California associated with great, classy wines such as "Insignia" and "Bacchus" produced by Phelps, "Opus One" by Mondavi/Rothschild and "Rubicon" by Coppola".

# 227

The word "estate" has a particular meaning in the United States. It refers to particular winegrowing estate, the term corresponding roughly to the French "Château".

228

The pricing of the finer Californian wines is high. The number of bottles produced is low and because of this the high price is justified to a certain degree, particularly in the case of the finest red wines for which Californian winegrowers are deservedly famous.

Many Californian white wines have a strong taste of wood that is not to everyone's taste. It may be acquired from the use of real wooden barrels, or merely from hanging small bags filled with oak wood chips in the steel vats; it is not always clear which.

229

When asked about the addition of oak wood chips to steel vats, winegrowers never answer "yes" or "no" but only that "some winegrowers do this".

230

The wine laws and classifications in South America are based on those used in Spain and Portugal. For instance, Argentina distinguishes between blended wines (vinos de corte), table wines (vinos comunos) and vintages (vinos finos), which are subjected to strict regulations. There is also differences within the various categories.

Although the winemakers of Australia, New Zealand and South Africa have adopted some of the regulations used in Europe, they do define wines geographically in the European manner.

# WINE AND VINTAGES

233

Assessing a wine on the basis of the
vintage is extremely difficult, because
most wine enthusiasts find it very hard
to judge the criteria that make up a good
vintage.

The same weather conditions that produce excellent wines in France or Italy may have catastrophic consequences elsewhere.

234

235

A good vintage often means different things for the winegrower and the consumer. A high yield of good but not first-class quality grapes is probably more important for most winegrowers than a low yield of excellent quality grapes making wine that is harder to sell because of its high price.

The quality of a wine depends first of all on the terroir, in other words the combination of climate, micro-climate, soil, its treatment and the situation of the vineyard. When all these conditions are fulfilled, great wines also require good year with good weather from the time the vines flower to the harvesting of the grapes.

236

237

In order to find out which vintages are special, it is best to consult specialist books and magazines. Besides Hugh Johnson's *Pocket Wine Book* , there are also wine magazines and gourmet magazines that list the best vintages and the ageing potential of the various wines.

# 238

Records of vintages usually go back a long time, especially in the case of port and red Bordeaux, because of their long ageing potential.

# 239

There are wine collectors who specialise in old wines and organise annual events when these old wines are served. The wines offered are influenced by the fact that wines of the best vintages keep longer than those of lesser years. The difference may be as long as several decades depending on the vintage.

**240**

If the wine has a slight bouquet of sherry, it is an indication of oxidation. The colour will confirm this: both red and white wines will tend towards a browner colour.

Oxidized wines are past their best although many a wine lover will enjoy something a little out of the ordinary.

**241**

## 242

The quality of wine can vary from one region to another in the same year. For instance, a good vintage in Bordeaux may happen in the same year as an unsatisfactory one in Burgundy.

243

Quality as well as quantity depend on weather, climate and soil. The amount of rainfall needed is not the same everywhere. For instance, in Andalusia too much rain will leach many of the minerals required by the Palomino grape from the calcareous soil, while loamy soil needs more water because much of the rainwater runs away without reaching the roots.

# 244

Nowadays the quantity of moisture can be regulated by irrigation in most regions (except in extreme drought), but the sun is beyond human control. Winegrowers may risk delaying the harvest so as to benefit from the last rays of the sun in order to increase the degree of sugar in the grapes.

# BUYING WINE AND WINE IN THE RESTAURANT

245

With fine wines, because so much depends on the vintage, it is important to find out as much as possible about particular vintages. The best tip is to find a wine merchant whom you can trust. A good wine merchant will advise the best purchases for your taste, requirements and budget.

Wine clubs are another way to build up a cellar. A wine club will send cases of wine to its members on a regular basis – against payment, of course.

The situation is different in a restaurant where the wine waiter should be consulted for guidance. There is no need to be shy because that is what he is there for, to help people choose the right wine to go with the dishes chosen from the menu.

247

248

Patrons of restaurants without a wine waiter will have to rely on the wine list, which should provide much the same information as the wine label.

**249**

With some exceptions, waiters in bars and pubs are not usually particularly knowledgeable about wine. The quality of the wines offered will depend on the management. If an enthusiast is in charge it should be good and interesting, but otherwise it will vary from the reliable but unexciting to the frankly poor.

**250**

Inevitably, a glass of wine in a bar will cost far more than the equivalent amount from a bottle of the same wine you have bought at retail. But the mark-up should not be exorbitant.

A selling price of three times the wholesale cost is common in the bar and restaurant trade. Staff costs, high rents and luxurious surroundings mean that an even higher mark-up is often applied. But there are some instances where inexpensive wine is sold at champagne prices with no justification. The customer should protest by going elsewhere next time.

251

House carafe wines in restaurants are usually inexpensive table wines or "vins de pays". They may be acceptable, but they sometimes try to exploit the name of famous regions, selling lesser wine more expensively than it is worth.

252

# 253

House wines often come from a barrel, wine box or other container larger than a bottle. This makes it harder to check on the quality, so you should still insist on tasting it first. Most serious restaurateurs will accept this. Otherwise, complain if it has a fault.

Naturally, the enjoyment of wine also depends on the atmosphere. If you find yourself in a Mexican restaurant you hardly expect to be served fine French wine, and if you were you would very likely find it unsatisfying. The choice of wine you are offered is likely to be much more satisfactory.

254

The fact is it all depends on the atmosphere. An inexpensive bottle of mass-produced wine with a spicy "chili con carne" will be very pleasant and you will not feel exploited.

**255**

**256**

It is certainly true that inexpensive wine need not be bad, and bargains are often found in supermarkets, particularly with special offers. But continuity of supply and of quality may be a problem.

# UTENSILS FROM CORKSCREWS TO GLASSES

257

The most important tool when drinking wine is the corkscrew. But which one is best?

**258**

The wine waiter's corkscrew folds up and looks like a pocket knife. Indeed it has a small knife to cut the foil and a spiral that is screwed into the cork in the normal way. A folding support at one end is then rested on the top of the bottleneck while the other end is lifted upwards to lever the cork out.

The ordinary T-shaped corkscrew relies on simple brute force to pull out the cork. The problem is that some corks are extremely stiff and often require great strength to open the bottle.

**259**

# 260

There are very expensive corkscrews that use a lever movement to plunge the screw into the cork and an upward one to remove it. This operation is then repeated away from the bottle, which automatically unscrews the cork from the spiral, making it ready for the next bottle. It is very quick, effective and convenient, but quite large and undeniably expensive.

The "butterfly" corkscrew is also very effective. It is screwed slowly into the cork and while doing so the two wing-like levers rise upwards automatically. The levers are then pushed down and the action removes the cork from the bottle.

261

262

An automatic corkscrew with a long spiral is simple but effective. There is a stationary part that rests on the bottle. Turning the T-shaped handle first winds the screw into the cork. It then "winds" the cork up it and out of the bottle. The two arms of the stationary part can then be squeezed together, gripping the cork and enabling the spiral to be unscrewed from it.

# 263

The spiral corkscrew has two handles, the first of which is used to drive the screw into the cork in the usual way. The second handle is attached to an anti-clockwise thread inside the outer part, which rests on the rim of the bottle. When turned, it smoothly lifts out the inner screw with the cork, removing it from the bottle.

## 264

The nervous should avoid corkscrews that pump air into the bottle through a hollow needle passed through cork until the air pressure pushes the cork out of the bottle.

## 265

The most unusual and least practical corkscrew is the sabre sword. In Tsarist Russia, officers at court are said to have opened Champagne with a blow of the sabre knocking the neck off the bottle.

266

If the cork is too tight, it can help to twist the corkscrew diagonally into the cork.

# 267

If the cork breaks in half while you are pulling it out, the rest of the cork can sometimes be removed by twisting the corkscrew diagonally into the remaining cork. If that does not work, the solution is to push the rest of the cork into the bottle. It may not be an elegant solution but it is the only way to get to the wine.

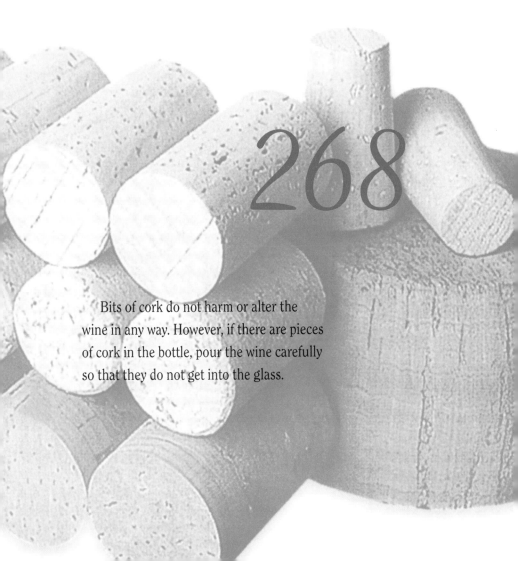

268

Bits of cork do not harm or alter the wine in any way. However, if there are pieces of cork in the bottle, pour the wine carefully so that they do not get into the glass.

269

Which wine in which glass? Let us start with Champagne. All sparkling wines are best served in flutes. These are much more satisfactory than the traditional flat champagne glasses of the past, which seem to have been designed to dissipate the bouquet and the bubbles as quickly as possible.

**270** Beware fashionable ways with drinks. Champagne and other sparkling wines have been served as a long drink on ice, which does it no good at all.

**271**

As well as diluting the wine by melting, the ice cubes drive the carbon dioxide out of the glass, thus making the wine flat in a very short time.

# 272

Cocktails made with sparkling wine, such as Buck's Fizz (sparkling wine and orange juice) or the Bellini (champagne and puréed white peaches) are also best served in flutes.

A type of glass that has become very popular for wine tasting is a larger version of the Spanish copita in which sherry is drunk. It is good for wine tasting because the tall, slightly tapering shape keeps the bouquet in the glass.

273

274

Most wine glasses are quite similar to each other as far as their basic shape is concerned. This is also true of white wine glasses which are approximately the same size as wine-tasting glasses, although in the case of the latter the rim is slightly curved towards the inside.

275

Red wine glasses are the same shape as white wine glasses but slightly larger.

276

Burgundy glasses are more balloon-shaped than the others so
as to allow the bouquet to develop as much as possible.

# 277

Once consumed, wine and water go together well. It is often recommended to order a bottle of mineral water with the wine. This will dilute the wine (in your stomach), and it will satisfy thirst. Drinking wine to quench the thirst is not effective.

# THE WINE TRADE

278

The wine trade gives employment many people in various fields outside that of winegrowing and winemaking, ranging from oenological research to wine retailing, wine tasting and wine journalism.

## 279

The **winegrower** is responsible for the vines, from the moment of planting to the picking of the grapes, and for looking after the vineyards all year round.

## 280

In many regions winegrowers take their grapes to **cooperatives**, which produce the wine and market it.

In some areas wine-growers themselves get together and form small associations producing modern wines with a reasonable quality-price ratio

281

282

PROHIBIDO
FUMAR

The traditional situation is changing fast. Young winegrowers in particular often have their own ideas and prefer making their own wine without the help of cooperatives.

# 283

In small wineries the owner is often also the *"maître de chai"*, looking after the production of the wine. But in a larger winery, there will be a specialist responsible for the cellar and its activities, dealing with the whole vinification process from the delivery of the grapes to the bottling of the wine.

Oenology is the science of wine, and an ***oenologist*** is an expert in all areas associated with growing grapes and making wine. They will often have been trained at famous wine schools such as Davis in California, Geisenheim in Germany, Rust in Austria or San Michele in Trentino. Large wineries often employ their own oenologist.

284

# 285

Consumers on the other hand will more often have dealings with the *"sommelier"*. These professional wine experts are usually employed in top restaurants and hotels.

# 286

As well as advising customers, sommeliers are also responsible for buying the wine. This is an enormous responsibility because it can involve sizable quantities of expensive wines. They deal with large sums of money and mistakes are rarely forgiven because wine ties up so much capital.

# 287

Sommeliers are often involved in composing the menu with the chef to ensure that the food and the wines offered should go together.

A **chef** should also be knowledgeable about wine because in restaurants without a sommelier, the chef must make sure that the wine selected by the customer "goes" with the sauce.

288

The **wine merchant** is the most important link between the winegrower or wine cooperative and the consumer. Some customers go directly to the winegrower but very few people are in a position to do this. Therefore the wine merchant is the person on whom the customer relies. Competence, honesty, frankness and the ability to inspire confidence are the characteristics required.

289

# 290

**Wine tasters** and **wine critics** are found in various professions associated with wine, including journalists, supermarket buyers, oenologists and sommeliers. They are all experts trying to help the layman understand and appreciate wine better.

# 291

Besides the bouquets and tastes of the classic grape varieties, there are some characteristics that may only apply to one wine in particular and to no other. This is an invaluable aid to recognition.

# BOUQUET AND TASTE

## 292

Wines containing Cabernet Sauvignon, either on its own or in blends, always have a distinctive taste of blackcurrants.

## 293

Wines have tastes and fragrances reminiscent of many everyday items, enabling them to be described in words. Examples include the fresh taste of apples, fruits of the forest and peaches, and a vast range of other descriptive similes.

**294**

For instance, the Austrian Grünen Veltliner grape has a distinctive peppery note that is specific to this kind of wine.

But there are limits: people who claim to be able to taste a difference between Williams pears and the skin of William pears, or between oysters and oyster shells are perhaps stretching credibility too far. They are however a much rarer phenomenon than is often suggested.

**295**

# 296

When you pour yourself a glass of wine, or someone pours one for you, you immediately know whether you like it or not. It is a good idea to try and work out why you like it or dislike it. This will help you decide what kind of wine to buy again or stock up on.

It is worth buying a bottle of a really good (but not absurdly expensive) wine occasionally, to provide a reminder of how excellent wine can be and the heights to which more ordinary wines aspire.

297

Naturally, laymen need a few basic criteria to guide them in their choice of wine. But to try and detect excessively complex and vague characteristics of wine can detract rather than add to the pleasure of wine drinking.

298

# WINE REGIONS OF THE WORLD

## 299

Vines are cultivated in many countries throughout the world but only a few countries boast a perfect climate. All too often the weather is too hot or too cold, too wet or too dry. It is true that vines adapt themselves to their environment, but if the terroir is not right, the yield will be poor in both quality and quantity.

# 300

The traditional winegrowing regions are situated in Europe. Although winegrowing was imported into Europe from Asia Minor, it was the Europeans, in particular the Greeks and Romans, who exercised the greatest influence on the development of winegrowing.

# 301

## Germany

**Saale-Unstrut** (Freyburg, Naumburg), **Sachsen** (Dresden, Meissen), **Ahr** (Ahrweiler, Bad Neuenahr), **Mittelrhein** (Koblenz, Bacherach), **Mosel-Saar-Ruwer** (Trier, Bernkastel-Kues), **Rheingau** (Eltville, Hochheim, Rüdesheim, Geisenheim), **Rheinhessen** (Nierstein, Nackenheim, Mainz), **Nahe** (Bad Kreuznach), **Franconia** (Würzburg, Iphofen, Sommerhausen, Randersacken), **Hessische Bergstrasse** (Bensheim, Heppenheim), **Pfalz** (Deidesheim, Neustadt, Bad Dürkheim), **Baden** (Breisach, Karlsruhe, Heidelberg, Durbach), **Württemberg** (Stuttgart, Heilbronn, Öhringen).

# 302

## France

These are the main wine regions and their most important cities. ***Champagne*** (Reims, Epernay, Ay), ***Alsace*** (Riquewihr, Colmar), ***Loire*** (Tours, Nantes, Angers), ***Burgundy (Bourgogne)*** (Macon, Beaune, Chablis), Jura, Savoie, Côte du Rhône (Avignon, Tornon), ***Bordeaux (Bodelais)***, ***Sud-Ouest*** (Pau, Bergerac, Cahors), ***Languedoc Roussillon (Le Midi)*** (Montpellier, Carcassone, Narbonne, Perpignan), ***Provence*** (Marseilles, Aix-en-Provence, St Tropez), ***Corsica***.

# 303

## Italy

Italy is divided into three wine regions: Northern Italy, Central Italy (including Tuscany) and Southern Italy, but in fact there are 20 individual wine regions.

# 304

Northern Italy includes:

**Südtirol** (Bolzano, Merano, Kaltern)

**Trentino** (Trento, Rovereto)

**Lombardy** (Milan)

**Aosta Valley**

**Piedmont** (Asti, Alba, Canelli)

**Veneto** (Venice, Vicenza, Verona)

**Friuli** (Udine, Trieste)

**Emilia Romagna** (Modena, San Marino, Bologna, Parma)

# 305

Central Italy:
***Tuscany*** (Florence, Siena, Chianti)
***Umbria*** (Perugia)
***Marches*** (Ancona)
***Latium*** (Rome)
***Abruzzi*** (Pescara)
and, south of the Abruzzi,
***Molise***

# 306

From a viticultural point of view Southern Italy starts in **Campania** (Naples). The other regions are **Apulia** (Bari, Taranto), **Basilicata** and **Calabria** (Reggio Calabria).

# 307

**Sardinia** and **Sicily** also have a long tradition of wine-making. The **Lipari Islands** to the north of Sicily produce some unusual wine specialities.

## Spain

Spain is the largest winegrowing country as far as the surface area covered with vineyards is concerned, almost one and a quarter million hectares of vineyards produce a large number of simple wines but also some outstanding wines which can compete with the best in the world.

The best wines come from northern Spain: **Navarre** (Pamplona), **Rioja** (Longrone), **Galicia** and its wine regions of **Rias Baixas**, **Bierzo** and **Valdeorras** (Santiago de Compostella), **Castile Léon** with the wine regions of **Rueda**, **Gigales** and **Ribera del Duero** (Salamanca, Valladolid), **Aragon** which includes the regions of **Calatayud** and **Carinena**, Catalonia includes the region of **Penedes** where most of the Cavas come from. South of Madrid is rthe region of **Castile La Mancha**. To the south-west are the wine regions of **Valencia** and **Murcia**. And right in the south is **Andalusia** with its sherry producing region. Wine is also produced in the **Canary Islands** and **Balearic Islands**.

# 310

## Portugal

**Vinho Verde** (to the north of Porto), the **Douro** region, which is famous for its great red wines as well as for its port wine (produced in the region to the weat of Porto), **Dao** (in the centre of northern Portugal), **Bairrada** (south of Porto), **Estremadura** (north of Lisbon). **Ribatejo** (to the north-east of the capital), **Setúbal** (to the south-east of Lisbon), **Alentejo** (to the east of Lisbon, on the Spanish border) and **Madeira**.

# Greece

To the north are the regions of **Macedonia** and **Thrace**. In the centre are **Thessaly** and **Epirus**, **Peloponnesus** (the best wines come from the mountainous wine-region around Patras). In addition, the **Greek islands** have a few special wines (such as Samos for instance).

*311*

_312_

## Turkey

Most Turkish wines come from the region around the **Sea of Marmara** and **Thrace**. Wine is also produced in the coastal regions of the **Black Sea**, the **Mediterranean** and **Aegean Sea** as well as in Anatolia.

# Israel, Lebanon, Cyprus, Algeria, Morocco, Tunisia and Egypt

These are all countries with an ancient tradition of winegrowing that has nearly disappeared after centuries of political riots. Today these countries produce wine mainly for export and the tourist industry.

**314**

Wine is also produced around the Black Sea. The *Ukraine*, *Georgia* and *Russia* – considered the cradle of wine-growing – produce rather average wines that are hardly ever exported.

## The Danube regions

**315**

The countries through which the Danube flows include *Hungary* (famous for Tokay and wine from the Balaton region), *Bulgaria*, *Romania*, *Czech Republic*, *Slovakia*, and *Slovenia*.

The best known region in the Balkans is **Amselfeld**. But wine production has come to end in this region because of the various wars of recent years, especially in Kosovo. Recently a few winegrowers have resumed production on a small scale. However, the figures are still far removed from those of the past (especially as far as export is concerned). It is still too dangerous to work in the vineyards, many of which have been sown with mines

316

# 317 Austria

Austria has no less than 15 winegrowing regions across the five provinces, Lower Austria, Burgenland, Vienna, Bergland Austria, Styria. In the north *Weinviertel* (Stockerau, Poysdorf), *Donauland* (St. Pölten), *Kamptal* (Langenlois), *Kremstal* (Krems), *Wachau* (Spitz, Dürnstein) and *Traisental*. In the centre *Vienna* (Grinzing, Nussdorf), *Carnuntum* (to the south-east of Vienna), the *Thermenregion* (Gumpoltskirchen, Baden), *Neusiedler See* (Neusiedle, Illmitz), *Neusiedler See – Hügelland* (Rust, Eisenstadt) and *Mittelburgenland*.

In southern Austria: **Südbur-genland**, **south-eastern Styria** (to the east of provincial capital of Graz, **western Styria** (to the west of Graz) and **southern Styria**.

318

## Switzerland

The seven wine regions are distributed across the three areas of Western Switzerland, Eastern Switzerland (the individual vineyards are scattered around the Bodensee and in the south between St. Gallen and Basel) and Southern Switzerland. They are **Graubünden** (Chur), **Ticino** (Bellinzona, Lugano), **Wallis** (on the Rhône), **Geneva**, **Waadtland** (Lausanne) and **Neuchâtel** (on the lake of the same name).

## Great Britain

As in Roman times, wine is now being produced again in England and Wales, particularly in Kent, Sussex, Surrey, Hampshire, the West Country and East Anglia.

320

# 321

"New World" wines are made in the Americas, South Africa and Australasia - in fact, anywhere outside Europe the Near East and North Africa. These "new world" countries produce great wines, many made from European grapes originally grown by European immigrants and their descendants.

## California

California is one of the most important wine producers, and it is the largest and most productive wine regions in the United States. It produces over 90% of all the wine bottled between Long Island and San Francisco.

**323** The best known regions are as follows. To the north of San Francisco: *Napa Valley, Sonoma Valley, Sonoma Coast, Russian River Valley, Knight's Valley, Dry Creek Valley, Alexander Valley, Clear Lake Valley, Anderson Valley* and *Potter Valley* in Mendocino County.

**324** Wine is also produced to the south of San Francisco in the vineyards of the Californian south coast stretching from San Luis Obispo as far as Los Angeles.

# 325

Wine is also produced further inland, in the region of the *Sierra Foothills* situated between Sacramento and Lake Tahoe and in the *Central Valley* around Fresno.

Oregon: **Williamette Valley** is the most important wine region in the state of Oregon. Although not right on the Pacific it benefits from its climate.

326

327

Washington State: The best-known regions are **Columbia Valley, Yakima Valley** and **Walla Walla** in the south.

# 328

The other wine regions of the United States are scattered across most of the country, but with a clear emphasis in the direction of the East Coast.

329

Wine is produced in the **Pennsylvania** and New England (particularly **Connecticut** and **Massachusetts**), **New Jersey** and **Maryland**.

Other famous American winegrowers are in **Texas, Tennessee** and **Georgia**.

330

331

## Canada

Wine is also produced in Canada, in a few parts of **Ontario**, **Nova Scotia**, **Quebec** and **British Columbia**.

# 332

## Australia

Australia is an extremely important winemaking country. The four wine regions in the south of the continent produce excellent wines: **Western Australia** (Perth), **Southern Australia** (Adelaide), **Victoria** (Melbourne) and **New South Wales** (Sydney, Canberra).

# New Zealand

The wine regions are distributed throughout the whole of the country, in both South Island and North Island. More wine is produced in the latter, where the most important wine regions are **_Auckland, Gisborne_** and **_Hawke's Bay_**. The main wine regions in South Island are **_Marlborough_** and **_Canterbury Christchurch_**.

333

# 334

## South Africa

South Africa has a long tradition of winegrowing. The main wine regions are around **Stellenbosch**, **Paarl** and in the district of **Constantia**.

# 335

## Chile

Chile is another celebrated winegrowing country. The most important wine regions are the ***Northern Region*** (Aconcagua and Casablanca), the ***Central Region*** (Santiago) which includes the most famous Chilean wine region, Maipo Valley, and the ***Southern Region*** (the Rapel, Curicó, Maule, Itata and Bio Bio valleys).

# 336

## Brazil

Brazil also produces wine – and not only Caipirinha. The three main regions are ***Sao Paolo, Rio Grande do Sul*** and ***Santa Santa Catarina.***

# 337

## Uruguay

Uruguay only has one comparatively small winegrowing region.

# 338

## Argentina

Argentina is one of the largest producers in the world and steak lovers between the jungle and Tierra del Fuego love nothing better than their strong red wine. The most important winegrowing areas are **Mendoza** (on the Chilean border), **Rio Negro** (to the south-west of Buenos Aires) and **San Juan**.

# 339

## Columbia, Bolivia, Paraguay, Ecuador and Peru

Small amounts of wine are produced in Columbia, Bolivia, Paraguay, Ecuador and Peru. However, most of the grapes grown are used to make brandy rather than wine.

# Mexico

**Baja California**, the long peninsula that projects into the Pacific, is the centre of wine production in the land of the Aztecs. It is true that the Spanish conquerors had already been aware of the fact that it was too hot to produce wine here. That is why Mexico's original inhabitants had preferred to distil schnapps and the well-known Mexican spirit, tequila.

340

# 341

The rest of the world: Grapes are grown in some unusual places in the world. For instance, the Chinese cultivate vines in the centre of Peking.

## India

Wine is even produced in India, particularly to the south-east of Bombay where winegrowers specialise in the production of sparkling wines.

342

## Japan

Japan also has a modest wine industry. It is made in one region only, Hokkaido, to the west of Tokyo.

343

# THE WINEMAKERS

Wine and wine-producer. The very greatest names in the wine world are known to most people and the mere mention of their names makes people prick their ears. However, there is a new generation of winegrowers who make no claim to fame but "only" produceexcellent wines – year after year.

344

The most famous wine name in the world is undoubtedly that of the ***Rothschild family*** from Bordeaux. Philippe de Rothschild and his father have been true ambassadors of fine wine throughout the world. Meanwhile, Philippine, the daughter, continues the family tradition.

345

# 346

The Rothschilds and the Californian winegrower **Robert Mondavi,** have founded a company together that produces one of the best Californian Cabernet Sauvignons, "Opus One". The company is run by the two families who also produce wine in Chile and promote winegrowing in Israel.

# 347

Robert Mondavi is the great man of Californian wine. It is thanks to him that California and its winegrowers is now considered one of the greatest wine-producing regions in the world.

# 348

Still in California, **Francis Ford Coppola**, the producer and director of films such as "The Godfather" and "Apocalypse Now", has turned his hobby into a profession. He is now more often to be found in the Napa Valley than in Hollywood. This is not surprising. since his **Niebaum-Coppola** winery (now incorporating the old Inglenook wine estate) has a turnover of several hundred million dollars.

# 349

The largest winery in the world is that of **Ernest & Julio Gallo** in Sonoma (although the headquarters are in Modesto), producing and selling 700 million bottles of wine every year.

# 350

There are some "interloper" winegrowers who play a very important part in Californian winegrowing. For instance, in the 1970s the former building contractor **Joseph Phelps** bought some small vineyards near St Helena in the north of the Napa Valley and now produces outstanding wines that have won and continue win many awards. Phelps is among the top 20 winegrowers in the world.

# 351

In France, it is above all the great Champagne Houses and their families who, together with the Rothschilds, have written the history of winemaking and its delights.

Like the French and the Americans, Spain and Italy also boast great winegrowing dynasties.

352

The owner of the largest and most important Spanish winery, **Miguel Torres,** and his family, have long been a living advertisement of their country. Torres also has vineyards abroad, many of them in Chile.

353

The **Chivite family** from Navarre are also famous winegrowers, being the second largest in Spain. The reputation of their wines reaches far beyond the borders of the Iberian peninsula.

354

# 355

The most famous winegrowers in Italy are probably the ***Antinori family,*** known especially for their outstanding Chianti, and the ground-breaking vino da tavola Tignanello. The family also owns vineyards in Orvieto.

The **Gancia family** in Piedmont are virtually synonymous with Asti Spumante. The winery which has been in the family for five generations and produces much of Italy's spumanti, with the Moscato grape as basic ingredient.

356

# 357

**Ferrari** is one of the most famous brand of sparkling wine in Italy, Talento Ferrari from the Trentino. Their top label is the outstanding Giulio Ferrari Riserva.

# 358

Besides the already internationally famous wine producers, a few independent winegrowers have emerged in recent years in Germany who have become known for their outstanding wines.

# 359

**Bernd Philippi** and his **Köhler-Rupprecht** winegrowing domain in the Palatinate has been in the family since the 17th century. Philippi produces excellent Riesling and his Cabernet Sauvignon are also first class, but certainly not cheap.

# 360

**_Gerhard Gutzler_**: This young winegrower from Rheinhessen is not only famous for his magnificent Chardonnays, Silvaner and Spätburgunder but also for distillates from marc and pomace. This is a hobby of his that has become a profession.

# 361

**Armin Diel**, the owner of the estate of the same name on the Nahe (Diel auf Burg Layen, Schlossgut) produces remarkable wines. He is also a celebrated restaurant critic and wine taster who is both controversial and acknowledged. Hugh Johnson has described his "eiswein" as having phenomenal quality.

***Hans Wirsching*** runs one of the largest wine estates in Franconia with one of the most famous vineyards of the region: Julius-Echter-Berg in Iphofen. He specialises in dry Silvaner and Riesling.

*362*

# 363

It is rather difficult to pick particularly interesting winegrowers in Austria because there are so many. For instance, ***Alois Kracher*** from Illmitz on the Niedlersee: produces the best sweet wine in the world and Robert Parker, the American wine guru, has given him the highest accolade with his excellent assessments.

# 364

**_Josef Jamek_** has recently withdrawn from the business, which is now run by his daughter and son-in-law. However, Jamek still remains the "grand old man" of the Austrian wine scene.

# 365

**Willi Brünlmayer** from Kamptal
is famous for his outstanding wines
and also because he was the first to
have produced organic wine.